Stories and Prayers at 'Five to Ten'

A Selection of the Daily Broadcasts

SEVENTH SERIES

EDITED BY THE REV.
RICHARD TATLOCK

LONDON
A. R. MOWBRAY & Co. LIMITED

First published in 1963

PRINTED IN GREAT BRITAIN BY
A. R. MOWBRAY & CO. LIMITED IN THE CITY OF OXFORD
3261

CONTENTS

THE letters which follow the title of each story are the initials of the author. The authors' names are:

Miss Eva Bestley, Miss B. Brookwood, Miss J. Carr, the Rev. A. M. Chirgwin, the Rev. C. J. Davey, Mr. D. T. Evans, the Rev. J. L. Garrington, the Rev. T. H. Holloway, the Rev. A. J. Lewis, Mr. J. D. MacLean, the Rev. A. Manley, Mrs. G. M. Mayo, Mrs. Natalie Moya, Mrs. F. E. Pettit, Mrs. Ethel Ramsay, Miss M. G. Rhodes, the Rev. R. Tatlock, Mrs. G. F. Thomson, Mr. Harold Tweedie, Mrs. E. M. Unsworth, the Rev. E. White.

STORIES AND PRAYERS AT 'FIVE TO TEN'

I

ST. THOMAS AQUINAS

ST. THOMAS AQUINAS[1] was one of the greatest of Christian theologians and philosophers. Although he lived in the thirteenth century, the way in which he used and developed the legacy of ancient learning is still considered remarkable, and many modern philosophers still draw their inspiration from his writings. Yet as well as being a great scholar, he was also venerated as a saint in his own lifetime.

On one occasion he was pacing up and down the cloister in the early morning sunshine, reading from some learned volume, when a lay brother hurrying by, called to him: 'Come along, brother. You are to be my companion in some business I have to transact.'

Thomas was well aware that the lay brother did not know who he was, for the brother was a stranger to the district, and obviously some mistake had been made. However, he closed his book and without a word followed the friar.

Throughout the day the heavily built, middle-aged scholar, accustomed only to the desk and choir stall, limped

[1] 1225–74: Feast day, March 8.

in the heat and dust of an Italian summer, behind the lay brother, who was strong, used to manual labour, and a fast walker.

Thomas followed him through the arcades and markets of Bologna, laden with vegetables and supplies of all sorts. At last, he was recognized by some gentlemen of the city who indignantly demanded of the lay brother: 'Are you aware who is accompanying you and carrying your parcels?'

'No,' replied the lay brother, for the Prior had told him to take as his companion the first friar he happened to meet. On hearing that the unknown companion was none other than the great Doctor, so universally revered, the poor lay brother was filled with confusion and humbly asked the great man's pardon.

'Brother,' answered Thomas, 'the only one at fault has been myself. I have been unable to keep up with you all day!'

To those who asked why he had not explained the mistake in the first place he said: 'In humility and obedience lies the perfection of the Christian life. By it man submits to man for the love of God, as God rendered himself obedient to men for their salvation.'

Prayer:
Help us, O Lord, to do all things for thy sake.

2

WILLIGIS

IN the ancient city of Mainz on the River Rhine in the year 1000 there lived a very good and faithful priest. He was the son of a wheelwright and had a very simple upbringing; but by his own perseverance and merit, he became a bishop of the Church. Bishop Willigis[1] was honoured and beloved by all the people of Mainz, though secretly some of them did not quite like the idea of bowing to the bishop when they met him. They knew that he had been brought up in a small cottage just like themselves. The good bishop heard about some of these murmurings and he reproved his people as kindly as he could for thinking too much about mere descent. But the people who felt themselves to be somewhat superior to the bishop were annoyed, and they decided that they would play a trick on him.

One night they got some chalk and drew pictures of great wheels on all the doors of his house. As the bishop was leaving the house early next morning for a service, he noticed the chalk marks on all the doors, and stood silent for a few moments looking at the drawing of the wheels.

His chaplain who was with him expected the bishop to fly into a rage. Instead, a gay smile spread over his face. He ordered a wheelwright to make him a plough wheel which he kept in his own room, in memory of his upbringing. Then he asked for a painter to be sent to him and told him to paint white wheels on a scarlet background, in the same place where the chalk wheels had been drawn on the doors. Underneath the wheels, he told the painter to write the words: 'Willigis Willigis! Just think what you have risen from!'

And ever since that time, white wheels on a red background have been the arms of the bishops of Mainz.

Prayer:

Grant us, O Lord, the grace of true humility.

[1] Pronounced *Villigis.*

3

WINIFRED HOLTBY

WHEN Winifred Holtby learned from a London specialist that she had not more than two months to live, she went quietly and alone to the country, to Monks Risborough, in Buckinghamshire.

She arrived in early spring and, on one of the coldest mornings, after a night of hard frost, she went for a walk to a farm farther up the hillside.

Arriving at the gate to the farmyard, she stopped and looked about her. Smoke from the farmhouse chimney curled lazily upwards in the keen morning air, and some little distance away she saw a water trough. The water in it was frozen over and several young lambs were gathered there leaping about and jostling each other as they vainly tried to drink. Cautiously, she moved over to it and broke the ice with her stick, and as she did so, she heard a voice saying in clear, measured tones: 'As poor, yet making many rich: as having nothing, and yet possessing all things.'

The voice was so distinct, so real, that she looked around, startled; but there was no one there. She was alone with the lambs, on the top of a quiet hill.

Suddenly, all her grief, all her bitterness and her feeling of frustration disappeared.

Writing later to a friend she called this experience 'My Conversion.'

Prayer:

Help us to be as poor, yet making many rich: as having nothing, and yet possessing all things; through the grace of our Lord Jesus Christ.

4

THE JEWISH SCULPTOR

THERE was once an eminent Jewish sculptor who lived in Paris; but after the Nazi occupation of France he went to live in America.

Here he held an exhibition of his work and earned much praise from the critics. A Dominican monk who went to see the statues was very much impressed, and later visited the artist when he was at work in his studio.

'I want you to carve a Virgin for my church,' said the monk.

The artist laid down his chisel in surprise.

'But don't you know I'm a Jew?' he asked in amazement.

'Well, if it doesn't disturb you, it doesn't disturb me,' replied the monk.

So the artist agreed to make an image of the Blessed Virgin. Day after day he worked in his studio chiselling away at a great block of marble. Then, one day, the monk decided to visit him to see how he was getting on.

'Is the Virgin finished yet?' he asked eagerly.

'No', laughed the artist. 'A statue such as I am making is not made in a week. Come again in two months' time.'

On the appointed day the monk arrived. The image was standing at one end of the room. The monk went up to it and crossed himself. Then he bowed his head and stood for a few moments in prayer. He then looked carefully at the statue and saw some writing on it.

'What is that writing?' he asked.

'Look closer and you will see,' replied the artist.

The monk examined it and saw the artist's name and his fingerprint and these words: The sculptor, a Jew, faithful

to the religion of his ancestors, has made this Virgin for the
better understanding of men so that the Spirit may prevail.

Prayer:
   Lord, give us the grace of charity and understanding.

5

THE OLD WOMAN AND THE ONION

ABOUT a hundred years ago, in Russia, there lived a
great writer called Dostoevsky.[1] This is one of the
fables he told.

There was once an old woman who was hated by all her
neighbours for her backbiting and uncharitable ways. She
had only done one good deed in the whole of her life, and
this was when she was weeding her garden and an old
beggar approached her.

'Give me something to eat for the love of heaven,' he
moaned piteously.

The old woman pulled up an onion and threw it at him.
'Take that!' she shouted. 'And be off!'

It was not really an act of kindness, but nevertheless her
Guardian Angel noted it down as a good deed.

When the old woman died she went straight to hell.
She floated about in a lake of fire with all the other lost
souls. She cried out for mercy and pity, but nobody
answered her.

Only her Guardian Angel pitied her. Was there nothing
he could do? Then—he remembered the onion she had
given to the beggar. So he took an onion and floated high
in heaven above the fiery lake holding it in his hand.

[1] 1821–81.

He called out to the woman: 'Here you are; take hold of this and I will pull you out.'

The old woman reached up and grasped the onion. Slowly and carefully the angel began to pull her up. However, all the other souls saw it too. They also reached up to grasp the onion. They pushed and struggled and fought to get hold of it. And the old woman lost her temper.

'Here, you lot,' she shouted, 'stop that! You're not having a share in it. That's my onion!'

And as soon as she said those words, the onion broke, and she fell back once more into the flames of hell.

Prayer:

Deliver us, O Lord, from hatred of others and from all uncharity.

6

ALBRECHT DÜRER

ALBRECHT DÜRER[1] and Franz Knigstein lived in Nuremburg. They had been friends from boyhood and shared the same passionate desire to become artists. For some years they studied together, but it became evident that whilst each had an intense love of art, only one, Albrecht, had the gift of communicating his genius to canvas. One day they agreed to make an etching of our Lord's Passion. The works were compared at various stages until at last they were finished.

Franz's picture was excellent in composition and detail, but lacked warmth and feeling; Albrecht's had life and beauty and the quality of inspiration.

[1] 1471–1528.

The comparison was so marked that Franz was almost heart-broken. Clasping his hands in despair he congratulated his friend and said: 'The good Lord gave me no such gift as yours. Perhaps He has some other duty for me to do.'

'Keep quite still a moment!' cried Albrecht, and Franz waited, his hands still registering the resignation which was in his soul.

Swiftly Albrecht pencilled a sketch. 'Your hands may never paint a picture,' he said, 'but they can certainly make one. Maybe they will reach out as an inspiration to other men.'

And thus it was that Albrecht Dürer's famous picture *Praying Hands* was given to the world and became an inspiration to countless men and women.

Prayer:

> I dare not choose my lot.
> I would not if I might.
> Choose thou for me, my God,
> So shall I walk aright.

7

FATHER MARIO BORELLI

A YOUNG Italian priest, Mario Borelli, was saddened by the number of gangsters and dishonest youths to be found in the streets of Naples. He decided that the only way to help these lads was to win their trust. So, after getting permission from a very reluctant Father Superior, he used to get out of his priestly garb in the evenings and change into ragged clothes, dirty shoes, and join in with a gang.

But was it his size or his fierce temper that caused the boys to nickname him 'Vesuvio'? He slept in the streets with them, and joined in all their activities, even thieving. He soon found that even the most hardened characters longed for affection, a home, and security.

One evening Vesuvio told the gang he had found a place where they could all go and live together, an old bombed-out church, which had been abandoned.

Between them they cleared the floor of all the rubble, and mended the gaping holes in the roof. It was not long before Vesuvio had installed a stove and taught the boys to prepare and cook first-class meals. Then came the day to which Father Borelli had looked forward to with some apprehension. Sooner or later he must reveal his identity, and one evening he arrived, dressed in his clerical clothes.

After a moment's silence, most of the boys roared with laughter, but one of them protested: 'Vesuvio, I'm not religious; but I don't think you ought to dress up as a priest: that is sacrilege.'

Father Borelli smiled. 'But I *am* a priest,' he said simply, wondering how the news would be accepted. He need not have worried.

One of the boys came forward, and took him by the hand. 'Then we will call you Don Vesuvio,' he grinned, 'but, you will stay with us, won't you?'

That is how 'The House of the Urchins' was founded.

Father Borelli taught his boys to read and write and say their prayers, and he has usually been able to find them jobs as well when the time has come for them to start work.

Prayer:

We thank Thee, Father, that we do not have a high-priest who cannot be touched with the feeling of our infirmities.

8

'AS POOR, YET MAKING MANY RICH'

MICHAEL YASHIRO[1] was born in Hokkaido, the most northern island of Japan, in the year 1900. His father, the Rev. Kinnosuke Yashiro, was of Samurai blood, that is to say, of the Japanese nobility, and when he became a Christian he was disinherited by his family.

In the early years of this century there was little money for the support of Christian clergy in Japan and the Yashiro family grew up in extreme poverty. As a schoolboy Michael sold newspapers, hunted birds, kept rabbits and made and sold ear muffs from their skins to help support his family during the long winters when the snow lay on the ground.

As a young man he went to China, where it was easier to make money, and became a fish pedlar. But he had always wanted to follow his father's example, and at last after many set-backs he was ordained and put in charge of a small congregation at Kobe.

Soon his outstanding qualities were noticed, and Bishop Basil Simpson decided that Yashiro should go to England for two years to study theology at the House of the Sacred Mission, Kelham.

The Japanese student duly arrived and assiduously devoted himself to his studies, but it was soon noticed that he went nowhere and spent nothing at all. At first his fellow students put this down to his language difficulties and his natural feeling of strangeness at being in a foreign country. But at the end of a whole year, when Yashiro's English had become quite excellent and he seemed quite at home here,

[1] Pronunciations: Yáhshirō; Hokídō; Kinósooki; Sámmoorī; ī rhymes with *eye*.

but still never went beyond the village, the Principal felt there was something amiss and questioned him.

The Japanese student admitted that Bishop Simpson had given him money for his expenses at Kelham, but on arriving he had managed to decipher a notice asking students to pay a certain sum for their board and lodging if they could afford it. The sum was exactly the amount that Bishop Simpson had given him, so he had handed it all in at the office. For over a year the young Japanese noble, and future Presiding Bishop of the Anglican Church in Japan, had not had a single penny in his pocket.

Prayer:

We bless Thee, O Lord, for thy saints who by their poverty make many rich.

9

THE MESSENGER STORK

A PASTOR in Northern Germany was surprised to find one day that a stork had made its nest on the roof of his house. His children began feeding it every day, and in time the stork became quite tame; but at the first sign of approaching cold weather it prepared to migrate to a warmer country. The children were very sad at the thought of losing their pet, but their parents consoled them with the assurance that the bird would surely return in the spring. But the children, still uneasy at the thought of the stork not being cared for during the long winter, decided to write a little note. Having sealed it, they fastened it to the bird's leg. The note said that the stork was very dear to them, and it begged the people in whose country it might spend the winter to be kind to their pet, and send it back to them in the spring. A few days later they sadly watched the stork wing its way towards sunnier skies.

When the warm weather came round again, the children watched day by day for the stork's return: and then, there it was, tame and gentle as ever. Great was the children's delight to discover, attached to its leg, a note addressed to them. It was from a missionary in Africa, stating that he had read the children's note, and had cared for the stork, and he thought that young people whose hearts had prompted them to provide for the comfort of a bird through the winter would be willing to help clothe and feed the destitute boys and girls of his mission. And so the migrating stork led these children in Europe to help the children in Africa.

Prayer:

We praise Thee, O Lord, for all the wonders of creation and providence.

10

THE LITTLE BLACK TEACHER

KASOVA was a little black girl, just twelve years old, and she lived in a native village far away from the Mission School. Nobody knew how she had heard about the missionaries, but one day she suddenly appeared at the Mission School and said she wanted to learn. She was very shy and backward and the teachers found it very hard to teach her. Sometimes they almost gave up in despair because she was so slow; but she kept on trying.

Then, after twelve months, just as suddenly as she had
come, Kasova decided to go. She took with her a Gospel
of St. John and a hymn-book. Some years passed and nothing was ever heard of the little girl who was so slow to
learn. Her village was a long way off and none of the
missionaries could find time to make the journey there.
Then, one day, four boys came to the mission school from
a village a long way away, that the missionaries had never
visited. Very proudly they said: 'We want to study. We
can read.' The teachers were doubtful, so the boys opened
a Bible and began to read. The missionaries were astonished.

'Where did you learn to read?' they asked.

'Kasova taught us,' they said.

Kasova with her hymn-book and Bible had gone back to
the village and taught the children to read the Gospel and
to sing the hymns she had learnt. People came from miles
around to hear the stories she read. It was such a wonderful
story that the missionaries decided to go to Kasova's village
and see for themselves.

When they went, they found that there were many
people in the village who had become Christians and were
waiting to be received into the Church.

Prayer:

Teach us, O Lord, that we too may teach others.

11

MARSHAL LYAUTEY

MARSHAL LYAUTEY[1] had been sent by his Government to subdue the wild, outlaw tribes of Morocco
and, after he had done so, he became its ruler in the name of

[1] Pronunciation: Leeōtay.

France. He was a great soldier—but an even greater peace-maker. He ruled the turbulent Moroccan tribes in the mountains with as much love and care as if he were their father. Indeed, many of them talked to him as if he really were. They brought him the problems that rose in their village councils and their family circles, and the Marshal was never without a word of understanding advice.

Lyautey knew, however, that it was not enough to care for men's present needs. In his own way he tried to build for the future. Whether or not he would ever see the results of his schemes in agriculture, town building, or road-making, he determined to prepare something better for those who would come after him.

On one trip he trekked out into a district where a fierce storm had ripped up a forest of gigantic cedar trees. The tribesmen had dragged them away for firewood, and all that was left was a desolate, ugly space. The Marshal called the Chief of the Forestry Department to him.

'You will be planting cedars here to take the place of those which have gone, I presume?'

The Forestry Officer smiled in a somewhat superior way. The Marshal was evidently not as clever as most people thought him!

'Sir,' he answered, 'I don't think you quite understand. It takes a thousand years to grow cedars like these!'

'Indeed,' replied Lyautey. 'A thousand years? Then, my good Monsieur Pierre, it is important that we begin at once!'

Prayer:

May we look to the future, O Lord, safe in thy keeping.

12

ROBERT MORRISON

WHEN Robert Morrison was accepted as a missionary to China in the year 1807, he was given this assignment: 'Acquire the Chinese language and translate the Holy Scriptures into the Chinese tongue.' Morrison was prepared to undertake this tremendous task, never previously attempted, despite the fact that he knew that there were conditions in China which made the assignment virtually suicidal.

The Chinese law of that time decreed that: 'Such Europeans as shall privately print books and establish preachers who shall propagate their religion shall have this to look to: the chief or principal one shall be executed.' And another law decreed that any Chinese subject caught teaching a foreigner the ancient language would be put to death by slow torture. Still, Morrison went forward and tried to secure a passage to China with the East India Company, to Canton, the only open port on the whole China coast. But the East India Company refused. They adhered strictly to the Chinese law barring all 'foreign religionists' so as to protect their own position and trade.

Morrison sailed to America to look for a ship's captain who would be willing to give him a passage. He approached a Mr. Blakeman, Captain of the *Trident*, but Blakeman did everything he could to dissuade the young Englishman. Morrison, however, would not be put off.

Still Blakeman kept on refusing, until, on the morning of the day he was to sail, in order to rid himself of the persistent young missionary, he heaped sarcasm on him, laughing at him, ridiculing his religion and his belief in his vocation.

'And so, Mr. Morrison,' he said, 'you really expect that you will make an impression on the idolatry of the great Chinese Empire?'

'No sir,' replied Morrison, 'but I expect God will.'

Captain Blakeman said no more, but when the *Trident* sailed out of New York harbour with the noon tide, Robert Morrison was hidden on board.

Prayer:

Grant us the fortitude, O Lord, to follow without fear wherever thy truth may lead.

13

THE CARMELITE

IT was rare indeed for a Jew to achieve any position of authority under the Nazi régime in Europe. But one Polish Jew actually became an officer in the Gestapo during the war. He had been picked from a youth organization because of his ruthless brutality.

One evening he was told by his superior officer that the Jewish quarter of the town was to be 'liquidated the following night.' At last the young Jew's conscience awoke, and under cover of darkness he warned his people. The old people did not believe him, but the young ones fled to the nearby forests.

The next night, after the killing and looting were over, the Jew and his superior officer were awaiting supper.

'Who could have warned them?' wondered the older man.

Sickened by what he had seen and done, the youth said: 'I did.'

The older man roared with laughter and slapped him on the back, sure that he was joking.

The Jew, however, excused himself on the pretence of looking for one of his fellow officers. Leaving the building he ran blindly through the streets, neither knowing nor caring where he was going, nor what he intended to do. Eventually he found himself in the dark, silent fields, and lay down and slept. By dawn the search was on and two parties of S.S. men passed within yards of him. Then, when darkness returned, he made his way to the convent of the Polish Sisters of the Resurrection, the only refuge he could think of.

The Reverend Mother looked at the S.S. uniform.

'You say you knock in the name of God. I will take the risk.' He was taken up to a disused attic where he remained for several months, and among the dusty books he found a Bible, which he read from cover to cover. At length he told the Reverend Mother that he wished to be baptized.

Soon afterwards the nuns were ordered to leave their convent and, dressed in a nun's habit, the former Gestapo officer went with them and joined a resistance movement in the forest organized by the young Jews whose lives he had saved.

And after the war he became a Carmelite friar.

Prayer:

Grant us the courage, O Lord, always to fulfil in action what we know to be right.

14

THE EMPEROR'S FOOL

A CHINESE emperor had a court jester who was the
very essence of stupidity. At last the emperor got so
impatient that he planned a long holiday for his jester. He
handed him a stick and ordered him to give it to whoever
was a bigger fool than himself.

For years the court jester wandered through many lands.
But he had a generous and humble heart and could never
decide that any one of his fellow human beings was more
stupid than himself. Old and broken by his failure to do as
he was bidden, he returned home to confess to his master
that he could find no one more stupid than himself. But
when he got back he found the emperor on his death-bed.

'I am going on a long, long journey,' the emperor told
him.

'Are you going beyond the far boundaries of your
empire?' asked the jester.

'Much farther,' said the emperor. 'The journey is so long
that I shall never return.'

'Have you made the necessary preparations for such a
long journey?' asked the jester. The emperor confessed
sadly that he was not in any way ready for this journey. But
the jester's face lit up. Only a much bigger fool than himself
would start on such a long journey without preparing for it.
So he bowed before his master and handed him the stick.

Prayer:

Bring us, O God, to know thy salvation in Jesus Christ
our Lord.

15

THE ROSE-BUSH AND THE APPLE-TREE

MANY scholars are of the opinion that when Jesus was a boy He came under the influence of a famous Rabbi whose name was Hillel. Hillel was without question one of God's saints. And he was a great scholar and teacher too. This is one of the parables he used to tell—and Jesus probably knew of it.

A rose-bush and an apple-tree grew side by side and, at the proper season, people would pluck the roses and pick the apples. But while they took the apples for granted and usually walked away, they would always linger by the rose-bush and admire its blooms and breathe in its exquisite scent.

And the rose-bush became proud and was filled with vainglory.

'Look at me,' it said to the apple-tree. 'Everyone admires me and loves my scent. You may be taller than I am; but what's that! You can never compare with me.'

'But I can,' said the apple-tree. 'I could compare with you even if you were taller than I am and were even more beautiful and fragrant than you are.'

'Oh,' said the rose-bush. 'And what secret virtue is it that makes *you* compare with *me*? It would be interesting to know.'

'It's a very simple thing,' replied the apple-tree. '*You* never give anyone a bloom unless you first prick them with your thorns: but I give my fruit without hurt even to those who cut me and throw stones at my branches. That is the virtue of kindliness. And kindliness is greater than beauty.'

Prayer:

Grant, O Father, that we may be kind one to another, tender-hearted, forgiving one another, even as Thou, for Christ's sake, hast forgiven us.

16

THE PLOUGHMEN

A LAWYER and a businessman decided that they would like to travel in other countries and joined a party that was going round the world. They were both members of the same Church and their minister was greatly interested in their tour. Before they set out he asked them to keep their eyes and ears open for any interesting things they might see or hear, especially in any of the countries where missionaries were at work. The men promised they would, little knowing that the journey would mean so much to them.

When they returned the lawyer took a rather curious photograph to the minister. It was a photograph of a boy pulling a rough plough in a field, while an older man held the handles and guided it.

'That old man taught me what sacrifice means,' said the lawyer, 'and I intend to double my subscription to the Church.'

The minister asked him what had happened.

It was in Korea, one day, that he and his friend saw the boy pulling the plough and because they were amused at it, the lawyer took a photograph of it.

'That's a curious picture,' said the lawyer to the missionary who was acting as interpreter. 'I suppose they are very poor.'

'Yes,' was the quiet answer. 'That is the family of Chi Noui.[1] When the church was being built they were eager to give something to it, but they had no money; so they sold their only ox and gave the money to the Church. This spring they are pulling the plough themselves.' The lawyer and his friend stood silent for a moment. Then the business-man said: 'That must have been a real sacrifice!'

'They didn't call it that,' said the missionary. 'They thought it was fortunate that they had an ox to sell.'

Prayer:

O Lord, teach us the grace of giving gladly.

17

THE REVENGE

AN Afghan tribesman was brought into a Mission Hospital seriously wounded. He had been attacked by men of another tribe who left him blinded and apparently dead. But he had been picked up by a passing traveller and brought to the Mission Hospital where he slowly showed signs of life. When the Doctor came to his bed, he cried out: 'Sahib! O Sahib, give me my sight, if only for a week, so that I can find the man who did this to me and kill him.'

'This is a Christian hospital,' said the Doctor, 'and our Master Christ tells us to forgive our enemies.'

'Those are good words, no doubt,' said the man, 'but still, I must have my revenge. My sight has been taken away, and my heart is filled with hate for the man who wounded me.'

[1] Pronunciation: Ky Nooee.

'Let me tell you a story,' said the Doctor. 'Some years ago the British Government sent a white man over these mountains. His name was Captain Connolly. He was accused of being a spy and thrown into prison. There he found another Englishman, and together they endured many hardships and privations. But Captain Connolly managed to secrete one precious possession, a small Prayer Book. The two men read it daily and were much comforted, and in the margin, in tiny letters, Captain Connolly wrote something of their life in captivity. They knew the end could not be far off, and, soon after, the two men died.

'One day, some months later, a Russian was walking through the streets of Bokhara in Central Asia. Among a pile of odds and ends in a shop he found a small English Prayer Book with writing in the margin of several pages. He could not read English, but he saw a name and address on the front page. Some impulse made him forward the little book to this address, and eventually it reached Captain Connolly's sister in England, and from those margin writings she gathered something of her brother's sufferings, and decided to have her revenge.'

'Ah yes,' cried the sick man. 'Revenge! What did she do?'

'She got together what money she could and she sent it to this hospital that a bed might be put here in memory of her brother. It is on that bed that you are now lying.'

Prayer:

Forgive us, O Lord, as we forgive those who trespass against us.

18

EDWARD RONDTHALER

EDWARD RONDTHALER was a young Moravian minister in the State of Pennsylvania. One Sunday evening he was appointed to preach in a little outlying country church. It was a wild and blustery evening. When he arrived there was no one inside the church. He lit the lamps and waited. The time came to begin the service, but still no one had turned up.

Edward Rondthaler had come to preach a sermon, and was determined to let nothing prevent him. He went up into the pulpit and began to tell the story of the Prodigal Son. As he drew near to the end of the sermon he proclaimed with great force: 'If there is anyone within the sound of my voice, let him accept *now* the forgiveness of the Lord.'

The door at the back of the church opened and a drenched unkempt figure walked slowly up the aisle. He too was a young man. 'How did you know I was there?' he asked the preacher as he reached the pulpit. 'I didn't make any noise in the porch.'

'I didn't know,' said Rondthaler, 'but you're very welcome.'

And then the story came out. Two days before, the young man had left his wife and two children. The responsibility of a family and the temper of his wife had been too much for him, and he had decided to leave home and start a new life somewhere else.

'But,' he told the preacher, 'I'm going back now. You've made me see what I've got to do ... and with God's forgiveness and help ... I'm going to do it. I'll make a new life with my wife and children.'

Twenty years later a very eminent divine came to preach in Edward Rondthaler's town, and the first person he went to see was Rondthaler himself.

'You don't know me, do you?' he said to Rondthaler.

'Well, I know of your great reputation.'

'Ah, but you don't know,' the visitor interrupted, 'that I'm the young man who answered the call of your sermon in an empty church, on a stormy night—twenty years ago!'

Prayer:

Lord, Thou dost never forget us: help us ever to remember Thee.

19

THE BAD-TEMPERED MAN

HANDED down from the Middle Ages is the story of a man who had a very bad temper.

But he was well aware of his fault: and he determined to do something about it.

He decided to escape from the company of those whose ways annoyed him and made him lose his temper. So he joined a monastery where he thought that among men of God he would be out of temptation's way.

But things did not quite work out as he had expected. After a while the monks began to annoy him with various little things they said and did, and he began to fly into tempers all over again.

So he decided to become a hermit. Better to live in solitude and peace—he thought—than live amongst men who made him lose his temper.

And he lived as a hermit for many long and lonely months. And then, one day . . .

He had just returned from the nearby well with his flask filled with water. It was made of glass and was completely round at the base. When he put it on the sand, he forgot to make a hole for it to stand in, and it fell over and the water ran away.

Quick as thought, he lost his temper and kicked the flask, which broke into a hundred pieces.

And in that moment he saw his own folly. He had not been trying to overcome his temper at all. He had been trying to run away from it. And he picked up his few belongings and started on the long journey back to his friends.

Prayer:

Help me, O God, to deal prudently with my faults, and not to run away from them, nor to put the blame on others.

20

BROTHER LEPER

THE road to the hospital was long and dusty and the ragged man who limped along it wondered if he would ever reach its cool doorway. He had come so far that he had lost count of the miles, and memories of his home village were already fading. The sun glared down on the scorching road and he knew there would be no shade until he reached the hospital. Surely, now that he was so near the end of the journey, his weary legs would not fail him!

He stumbled at last up the slope, until from somewhere he felt hands grasping his, and he was lifted bodily and carried inside. The coolness and freshness of the hospital cleared his delirium for a while, long enough for him to protest as the doctor began to rub ointment into his sores. He had really come to beg for poison to escape from the miserable life of a leper, he had no desire to live now! But already the ointment was soothing some of the pain and he sank back on to the bed.

There was a Mohammedan visitor watching the doctor, and he was amazed when he saw how carefully and almost lovingly the doctor cleansed and dressed the terrible sores on the leper's body.

'I cannot understand how you can touch a leper like that,' he said.

'Surely you would do the same for your brother,' said the doctor.

'Perhaps,' was the reply, 'but this man is not your brother, he is just an outcast and a leper, and he is black and you are white.'

'True, but God is my Father, and his, so we are brothers. And Jesus said: "As ye have done it to one of these my brethren, you have done it unto me."'

'If you believe that,' said the other, 'then nothing is too hard for you to do.'

Prayer:

Jesus said: 'Inasmuch as ye have done it unto these ye have done it unto me.'

21

THE MOSQUE OF NUR JEHAN

KASHMIR is a lovely country. Its swift-running rivers are white with the icy snow waters from the Himalayas. Long lines of poplars stand along the edges of the emerald green rice-fields, and wherever you look, the domes and turrets of the Mohammedan mosques rise towards the sky.

Every Friday, in their two's and three's or in their hundreds, men go to pray in these mosques. Five times, every day of the week, devout Moslems are to be seen saying their prayers, by the roadside, outside their shops or in their homes, their faces towards Mecca.

But there is one mosque where men have never prayed. It has never been used for worship since the day it was built. It is the Mosque of Nur Jehan.

Nur Jehan was an empress in India in the days when the first Elizabeth was Queen of England. Year by year the Moghul rulers went from the hot plains of India to the cool of Kashmir to escape the fierceness of the summer, and there they built palaces and gardens, like the Shalimar, which you can still walk in today. Nur Jehan, however, wanted to do something more than this, something that would make her famous for all time. After a good deal of thought, she decided to build a mosque for the worship of God.

When it was finished, men came to it from all over Kashmir and the great courtyard was crowded with worshippers awaiting the arrival of the empress. At last she arrived, in her silk and brocade, and the chief mullah stepped forward to thank her for her generosity in building so lovely a place of worship. As he spoke, the empress smiled.

She stretched out her foot, so that the people could see the jewels sewn into her sandals.

'It is nothing,' she answered with a shrug. 'These shoes cost more than the mosque.'

There was a moment of silence. Then, without a word in reply, the mullah led the worshippers out of the mosque, never to enter it again.

Prayer:
Teach us, O Lord, to withhold no gift from Thee.

22

WILSON CARLILE

WHEN Wilson Carlile was a young man he helped to arrange some meetings for the great preacher, D. L. Moody. Just before one meeting Moody was told that the building was full and they were turning people away. He came into the hall and asked why there were two chairs vacant on the platform. Wilson Carlile said that they were reserved for two particularly important and influential members of the committee. To which Moody replied that the meeting was not held for the benefit of the committee. 'Go out into the streets,' he said, 'and get the two worst people you can find and put them in those seats.'

That was a lesson Carlile never forgot.

As a young curate in Kensington Carlile began open-air preaching. The crowds came all right: the police reported that traffic was being held up, and one respectable church-goer wrote to the rector saying: 'Dear Sir, I was at your curate's meeting last night for five minutes. In that time three purses and two watches were stolen: can't you stop this nuisance?' But Carlile convinced the rector that the chap who will pick your pocket is exactly the man the Church ought to preach to; and he carried on.

One night when he answered a knock on the door, he found a man very uncomfortably standing on the rectory doorstep. He followed Carlile into the study and put on to his desk a wooden box which he had been carrying. Huskily he said: 'You take it, guv'nor. Look after it for me, I can't trust myself with it.'

Carlile undid the latch and lifted the lid and found himself looking at a complete set of burglar's tools and equipment.

He said to his visitor: 'No, don't trust me with it, either; but I'll show you a place where it will be safe.'

Through the dark streets they went together, and into the old church, down the aisle and up the chancel steps, right up to the altar. Carlile stooped and pulled the frontal to one side. He put the box on the floor beneath the altar and pushed it along until it was directly under the cross.

Prayer:

O Lord, help us to have compassion on all men for Christ's sake.

23

HIS SERVANT

ONE day, during the war, Miss Adams—welfare worker in a London factory—was sitting in her office when in burst an irate foreman. Without announcing his department, he said: 'It's Elsie. I've just about had enough of her

C

tempers! She ought to be given her cards! I'll not stand her cheek any more. Will you see her, ma'am?'

'Certainly. Send her,' came the reply.

Within a few moments an angry looking young woman came into the office. She did not give the welfare worker time to say anything, but started: 'All right, I've got me cards. So what!'

She was surprised not to receive a similar response, but instead, asked to sit down.

'Elsie, what do you do when you get home at night?' inquired Miss Adams.

'My mother's bedridden, so I see to her, do the room, and then sit by the fire.'

'When do you go to bed?'

'Bed? What, with all them bombs droppin'? No thank you! I've not been in bed for the last four months. I've got to be ready to help Mum.'

The welfare worker looked at Elsie.

'Thank you,' she said. 'That explains a lot. I'll try and get your hours shortened. There's nothing wrong with you. You're just tired. Do you think you could apologize to the foreman?'

Elsie relaxed, and looking up, she said: 'Crikey, you must be God himself!'

'No,' came the quiet reply, 'just one of his servants.'

Prayer:

Help us, O Lord, to understand other people for Christ's sake.

24

EVELYN UNDERHILL

ALTHOUGH Evelyn Underhill had lectured hundreds of times to adults and students, she had had very little experience with children, for she had none of her own. It was therefore rather an ordeal for her when, towards the end of her life, she was invited one morning during the war to take a Sunday School class in a Sussex village.

It was a lovely Spring day, and as she walked along the lane that led to the church, she paused every now and then to listen to the songs of birds and to inhale the sweetly-scented air. It was in such sharp contrast to the London she had just left. She had come south to rest from the bombing for a few weeks. In London, during weeks of blitz, there had been noise and stench, fear and disorder. Here was beauty and order and peace and loveliness. London smelt of fire and death and corruption. But Sussex, that beautiful day, was full of the scent of primroses and violets, and lambs were romping at the foot of the Downs.

Evelyn's warm heart went out to the little evacuees she was about to address. How lovely God's world was, and how hideously man was destroying it.

She opened the door of the little church and entered. She had decided to begin with a rousing hymn of praise. The children responded and sang well. When the singing was done, and they had all settled down into their seats, Evelyn Underhill asked them if they knew why it was that they should sing praises to God.

For a moment there was silence, then—'I know,' piped up a young Cockney voice eagerly, 'we sing to cheer God up.'

Prayer:

May we please Thee, Father, by doing thy will.

25

DOMINIC SAVIO

DOMINIC SAVIO was born in 1842 of Italian parents who could neither read nor write, but this did not prevent them from teaching their child the principles of their religion, which they knew by heart and practised devoutly.

Dominic's pleasing personality and intelligence soon attracted the interest of the village priest who sent him to a school in Turin when he was twelve. Here, in spite of delicate health, he was popular and soon took a leading part both at work and at games.

But when he had been at the school some months he heard a sermon which produced a dramatic change in him. The preacher spoke of the necessity for everybody to become saints, even schoolboys.

'It is God's will,' he said, 'that everyone should become a saint, and it is not very difficult if you are determined to make the best use of the graces which God bestows so abundantly on us all.'

'You boys can become saints,' he concluded, 'just by living your everyday lives as perfectly as you can. Not only by studying and praying, and by regular use of the Holy Sacraments, but also by joining in all the fun and games. Holiness for you lies in being happy and helping others to be happy.'

Dominic at once began to put this sermon into practice with great determination, and soon his influence over the other boys became very great.

On one occasion two of his friends developed a sudden hatred for one another and arranged to fight a duel with stones. Dominic heard of this and was present at the duel. He asked them if they would accept a suggestion. They agreed. Kneeling down between them Dominic suggested that they should begin their duel by each throwing their first stone at him, and saying aloud as they threw it: 'Jesus Christ who was sinless, died forgiving his enemies, but I who am sinful refuse to forgive an insult.'

The boys gazed at him in horror, for he was loved and respected by both of them, and it was not long before they were the best of friends again.

Dominic was only fifteen when he died, but he had carried out the duties of his life as a schoolboy so perfectly that he was recognized by his church as a Saint.

Prayer:

May our prayers and our Communions transform our daily lives.

26

DOING THE RIGHT THING

THERE was once a man who made up his mind one fine day to go to market with his donkey and his little son.

They had to set off early, because the market was held in a distant town, and the father decided that *he* would ride the donkey and the little boy could walk.

They had not gone very far when they met two men coming in the opposite direction and heard one of them say to the other: 'That's a fine thing. The big man rides and the little boy walks. He ought to be ashamed of himself.'

So the father dismounted, put his son on the donkey, and started to walk himself.

They had not gone far when they met a man and his wife and heard the man say: 'I don't know what the younger generation is coming to. The boy rides the donkey and makes his father walk.'

So the father took his son off the donkey and they all three began to walk.

They had not gone very far when they met two women, and one of the women said to the other: 'There's a couple of nincompoops for you. A perfectly good donkey, and they're *both* walking.'

So the father and the boy both mounted the donkey and began to hope that they would soon get to the market.

But they had not gone very far when they met two more men.

'Just look at that,' said one to the other. 'Two healthy people, with perfectly good legs of their own, too lazy to walk. They ought to be ashamed of themselves.'

The father was beginning to be rather puzzled by all this. It was wrong if *he* walked, wrong if the *boy* walked, wrong if they *both* walked, and just as wrong if *neither* of them walked. There was only one thing to do—they would carry the donkey! And carry the donkey they did, all the way to market.

But when they arrived at the market town, the entire population—or so it seemed—turned out to jeer at them.

So the father turned philosopher, and made this experience the opportunity for a sermon.

'Son,' he said, 'it turns out that we have been attempting to achieve what is not possible. We have made the mistake of trying to please everybody.'

And on the way home they took it in turns to ride and walk, and took no notice of anybody.

Prayer:

Though we shall never please everybody, O Lord, let it be our one concern to please Thee.

27

ABBOT MOSES

ONCE, long ago in the desert, temptation came upon a brother in a monastery and he fell into sin.

Many of the brethren were for casting him out of their midst, but there were some amongst the older monks who considered that at least he should first be tried and judged.

Accordingly, word was sent to a holy abbot named Moses, asking him if he would come and preside over the assembly that was to judge the sinful monk; but the abbot Moses refused. The brethren sent again, begging that he would come, but again he refused. Finally, they sent one of their number to tell him that the whole assembly was waiting for him and counted so much on his presence that they would not begin without him.

So then the Abbot Moses consented. But, before setting out, he procured an old and very large basket which he filled with sand and, as he went along, he carried it on his back.

The brethren who were waiting for him saw from a distance the holy old man bent double under his load and ran to meet him. But when they wanted to relieve him of the weight he said: 'No, I must carry my burden myself.' And he continued to walk on.

Then the brethren saw that a trail of sand was pouring from the basket and they said to him: 'Father, what does this mean?'

The old man answered: 'My sins are running out behind me and I do not see them. Yet am I come here to sit in judgement on another man.'

When they heard this, the brethren were ashamed of their lack of charity and said nothing to the guilty brother, but forgave him.

Prayer:

Forgive us our trespasses, O Lord, and make us merciful to the failings of our neighbours.

28

ARNOLD JANSSEN

DURING the Franco-Prussian war of 1870 political and religious conditions were unsettled and as a result German Christians were doing very little for missionary work abroad.

Arnold Janssen[1] was travelling throughout the country trying to interest his fellow clergy in missions, but it was no use. And now that he had come to Cologne, he found that the word had already gone round that Janssen 'wants to build a college for the missions; he hasn't tuppence to his name; he must be either a saint or a fool.'

Jansssen knew he was not a saint, and he began to wonder if he were not a fool; but he had taken his degree in the year that Darwin's *Origin of Species* had burst upon a

[1] Pronunciation: Yanssen.

drowsing world, and he foresaw a great decline in faith and felt that Christians must be prepared to fight it. What is more he recognized his own limitations. He had neither money, influence, nor administrative experience, and had never seen himself as a founder of a great new missionary college, only as its humble advocate.

He could get no help in Cologne, and he paced the streets in a fever of indecision. Should he give up and confine his preaching of the Gospel to the small community whose chaplain he was? He knew that this scheme of his was essential, but how or *where* could he get the power to do it?

He stood still in the busy street. In his mind's eye he saw his old father, now bent after a lifetime at the plough, saying the evening prayers. Every night as long as he could remember the old man had begun by reading the first verse of St. John's Gospel: 'In the beginning was the Word, and the Word was with God and the Word was God.' He always claimed that this verse was itself a great and powerful prayer and would always recite it if ever disaster threatened.

A great peace came upon the son as he remembered his father's faith. He knew now what he would do. He had seen a derelict inn for sale. He could just raise the purchase price. This would be his college. Two students had promised to join him, and they would be the nucleus of his missionary society. It would be called the 'Society of the Divine Word.' And the rest he would leave to God.

To-day Father Janssen's missionaries are to be found in every quarter of the globe.

Prayer:

Grant that the Church may be purged of the sin of idle words, and may not say one thing and do another.

29

THE SLAVE GIRL AND HER BOOK

A WOMAN slave-owner one day went down to the slave-market near her home to buy two or three more slaves. She walked round the market, looking at the ones that were up for sale, examining them, feeling their muscles, and asking what the price of each one was. As she was doing this she came to one slave, a young girl in her 'teens, who suddenly leaned forward and said: 'Buy *me*; please buy *me*; *please* buy *me*.'

The slave owner was rather taken aback; but she liked the look of the girl and decided to buy her (with two or three others) and then took them away to her home in the hills nearby. When she arrived home she sent most of them out into the fields to work, but she decided to keep this little girl in the house as a kind of personal and domestic slave.

The girl was a good, quick worker, and every day when her work was done she would take a book from under her shawl and curl up in a corner and begin to read. One day, her mistress found her reading and said in surprise: 'Can *you* read?'

'Yes,' replied the little girl. 'Can't you?'

'No,' said the mistress. 'Can you teach me?'

There and then the slave-owner sat down by her slave and had her first lesson in reading. The lesson-book that they used was the little girl's Bible, which was the only book in the house. The mistress proved a good pupil and before long she too was reading for herself. They read through the whole of the four Gospels together, some parts more than once.

In time, the book began to make its impression on the mistress. She became a different person and she also asked some of her neighbours to come in and join them for the readings.

Day after day the readings went on and soon the whole neighbourhood knew about them.

To-day there is a thriving Christian church in that town, and its real founder, under God, was the little slave girl who in the slave market had called out: 'Buy me; please buy me.'

Prayer:

Thanks be to Thee, O Christ, for the power of thy holy Gospel.

30

THE ISLAND OF MAKKAUR

THE island of Makkaur,[1] off northern Norway, is remarkable in several respects. It has no beach or harbour, and people arriving at, or departing from, the island do so by means of an iron ladder set against the cliff face.

For generations the one hundred odd people of all ages who lived in the one small fishing village had no church, and until about seventy-five years ago they had neither field nor garden, for there was no soil on the island. How the people of Makkaur came to possess both a church and soil is the story of one family's determination and courage.

It all began when a fisherman named Hansen[2] brought a few pounds of soil back to the island on his way home from a visit to the mainland. For some months he carried on the

[1] Pronunciation: Mākour.   [2] Pronunciation: Hānssen.

work single-handed, but later he was helped by his wife, Petroline. Together they rowed their small boat to and fro between the island and the mainland, each time bringing back a boatload of soil which they carried up the iron ladder, and spread out upon the rocks. For years the work went on, until there was enough soil to make one small field sufficient for one cow. Hansen died but Petroline, assisted by her son Bernhard,[1] carried on bringing in more soil until the field was large enough to support two cows.

Then, one day, Petroline decided that the time had come to build the church which she had long dreamt of seeing set up on the island. Quietly, she cleared a small area of ground near her field and she said to her son: 'Here our church shall stand.'

For the remainder of her life Petroline worked and watched her son and the villagers building her church. Her great desire was that her son, himself now an old man, might live to see the work completed. Petroline died, but her wish was granted. The church which she had laboured to build was consecrated by Bishop Berggrav[2] in the presence of Bernhard Hansen and the assembled villagers.

The altar candles were lit and thirteen children were baptized.

Prayer:

Grant, O Lord, with Thee beside us, with joy to persevere.

[1] Pronunciation: Bairnhaard.   [2] Pronunciation: Bairg-graav.

31

'STICKS' AND 'GINGER'

IT was a Wednesday evening in the East End of London and a crowd of small boys and girls were pouring out of a mission hall waving tickets in their hands. They were tickets for the annual trip to Southend on the following Saturday.

'What's the matter with Ginger?' asked a long-legged boy whose nickname was 'Sticks,' pointing to a small boy sitting on a doorstep crying.

'Oh, he's had bad luck. He came just too late. When he got to the hall all the tickets had been given out.'

'Hard luck,' said Sticks and then passed on.

But Sticks could not forget little Ginger crying on the doorstep. And an hour or so later he wandered down the street where Ginger lived and found him playing with the other boys there.

'I say, Ginger,' shouted Sticks. 'Would you like to go to Southend on Saturday?'

'You bet I would!' Ginger replied.

'Well, here's a ticket. I got it at the hall this evening but I can't go.'

Ginger did not ask any awkward questions about why Sticks could not go, but just took the ticket and ran shouting into the house to show his mother what Sticks had given him.

When Saturday morning came and they were all gathered on the railway platform the Superintendent of the Mission Hall noticed that Ginger was there and that he had a ticket in his hand. He also noticed that Sticks had failed to put in an appearance.

When he saw Sticks the next day he went over to him and said quietly: 'Ginger had a grand time yesterday.'

Prayer:

Inasmuch as you did it to one of your smallest brothers, you have done it to me.

32

THE GLADIATORS

BY the year 400 there were many people in Italy who disapproved of the cruelty of the gladiatorial combats, which were still one of the regular entertainments at Rome. Plenty of people had begun to say: 'Why doesn't somebody do something to stop this?' But nobody had got to the point of doing anything about it himself.

'After all, what can we do?' they said. 'Who would take any notice of us? The games are far too popular to be stopped by the protest of a small Christian minority.'

But Telemachus did not agree. He was determined to do something to try to stop this wanton bloodshed, and the cruel pleasure of those whose delight it was to watch the games.

First of all he tried to get an audience of the Emperor Honorius. But he had no friend at court: nobody took his request seriously: the emperor remained beyond his reach.

Next he tried to organize a public protest: he spoke to people in the streets of Rome and tried to stir them up— but all to no avail.

And so he had to make his protest all alone. He went to a combat. But instead of staying with the spectators round the ring, he walked right into the arena and began to try to separate the combatants. The crowd was furious. They cursed him and abused him. And, when he took no notice of their shouts, they took up stones and battered him to death.

When the story came to the ears of the Emperor Honorius, he commanded that Telemachus' name be recorded among the noble army of martyrs, and that the gladiatorial combats be forthwith excluded from the games.

Prayer:

We ask, O Lord, for the wisdom to distinguish the evils that should be changed, and for the courage to fight them to the end.

33

LORD SHAFTESBURY'S TEACHER

MARIA MILLIS would never have considered herself important. She was a simple woman, housekeeper to a family where the father, a busy member of Parliament, and his wife were always attending social functions, or engaged in other evening activities in which the husband's work involved them.

Maria Millis rarely saw her employers in the evening. They were always out. Their little son hardly ever saw them either. He was tucked away in bed—often lonely, and a little lost for love.

But Maria made up for those empty spaces in his life. She would creep to his room, read to him, and tell him stories from the Bible.

The boy never forgot those days, and when Maria died, he felt he had lost his only friend.

Maria Millis may not have been important to anyone but a lonely little boy. But Anthony Ashley Cooper heard the word of God from the lips of this humble woman, and when, as Lord Shaftesbury, he died, there were thousands who remembered him with deep affection and gratitude.

And like Maria Millis, the mainspring of all his activities was a simple yet powerful love for Jesus Christ.

Prayer:

Help us, O Lord, by serving Thee to serve all men.